THE

CABINETMAKER'S

WINDOW

POEMS

Steve Scafidi

Louisiana State University Press

Baton Rouge

Published by Louisiana State University Press
Copyright © 2014 by Steve Scafidi
All rights reserved
Manufactured in the United States of America
LSU Press Paperback Original
First printing

Designer: Laura Roubique Gleason
Typeface: Fournier MT

LIBRARY OF CONGRESS CATALOGING-IN-PUBLICATION DATA

Scafidi, Steve.
   [Poems. Selections]
   The Cabinetmaker's Window : poems / Steve Scafidi.
      pages cm — (Southern Messenger Poets)
   "LSU Press Paperback Original"—T.p. verso.
   ISBN 978-0-8071-5449-6 (paperback : alk. paper) —
ISBN 978-0-8071-5450-2 (pdf) — ISBN 978-0-8071-5451-9 (epub) —
ISBN 978-0-8071-5452-6 (mobi)
   I. Title.
   PS3569.C247A* 2013
   811'.54—dc23

                                              2013018876

THE CABINETMAKER'S WINDOW

Southern Messenger Poets

Dave Smith, *Series Editor*

For Elijah Luther and Isabella Daria,

my children,

And in memory of Donovan Blaise Kelly,

their grandfather, 1941–2013.

CONTENTS

3

4

I

Sometimes There Is a Shit Smell Everywhere

When a breeze catches fumes rising from a crack
in the septic and hoo-ee we say who was that.
Sometimes skunks fight under the floorboards

at night and when you walk in—in the morning
you begin to reek of it and by the end of the day
you are fouled with that deep musk of skunk.

And sometimes sanding a small eucalyptus box
made in China 100 years ago the astringency of
the medicine tree fills the barn and clears your head.

We cook chicken and beans, venison stew and corn
bread and sausage and Bill's wife sent him to work
today with three shrimps covered in coconut sauce.

But mostly it is coffee in the air or the peppery
sharp odor of sawn walnut that smells purple.
Mahogany dust has little claws that tear your eyes

and grip at your insides and sometimes we get what
is called ass-pine which stinks when you cut it
and you have to run away a little and say damn.

But since I was a boy it is another smell—the ordinary
fragrance of this place like the pews of a chapel,
something sober and holy despite the cat piss or

all of the things we say. It smells like light mostly,
what stained glass looks like—like a story being told.
The one where you live in one place until you die.

The West Virginia Copper-Wing

An apple falls through the branches of the tree
   and a green snake rises up flying
      with little wings iridescent

as the evening begins in the orchard
   on the edge of town. Three deer
      whisper grazing in the lane.

You could be eleven or twelve
   standing with a stillness you have
      never before known, a halo

of gnats around your head and this
   could be any year in recorded history
      of human life. No one

ever exactly remembers this moment
   or the next. We find ourselves
      in a royal pause and then we go on

asking what's next. We fall
   toward sorrow and we forget.
      Someone captures the miraculous

green snake with a net—
   pins it to a board. Someone
      sharpens a knife at the center

of the earth and it sounds like a wheel.
   Houses appear. Thousands
      of windows twinkle suddenly in

the settling dark. Stillness,
    which was the god of being
        eleven or twelve on the edge of town

just before someone you love
    calls you home and home being
        the god of this place, disappears.

All of it disappears and you are left
    lost in the majestic green clockwork
        that is next.

This Page

When the shop comes down
and there is nothing left
of the house I love
and the last fragment
of this page is eaten
by a beetle as it hoves
back down into the earth
to sleep away the sunlight,
the ruins of this place will
still cast shadows for a time
and the small blue crow
that swoops down out
of the willow will taste
the clickety scratch of
barbed legs working
against its throat and be
satisfied moving along
by wing and by song to
fly through the world
we had thought enough
once to find a way to praise.
However little good it did
light still falls across the page.

Song for the Holy Ghost

Thanks for the letter B and the long E.
Thanks for meaning most. And shouts
of what could be rage or joy I don't
know that rumble in the sky and grow
ominous and close. I know it is thunder.
Thank you for lightning over the house
and the sky-high towers of rain leaning
in the field and falling. Thank you
for the shimmer in the walls of heat
the storm breaks just before dinner
so my daughter puts on a sweater
before we eat. Thank you for the lovely
gift of her and all the time we had
that will go on I'm certain in the summer
of what will never pass. Something radiates
in all we were so that we are I hope
what lasts. *Love,* you are my only word
it seems. You have made me difficult
to be taken seriously by most. You
spill the blood of Being all over the Host.
You take the god of Death who wanders
out through space like an old woman
out for pancakes. You make the house
tremble in the storm until the heat breaks
and we sit down my family in the summer
in our sweaters and saying so makes it
better. Whoever You Are, watch out
for her. Protect her. She has a golden
secret like a soul to say. You should let her.

Two Cabinetmakers

Here's one—got a Mohawk hairdo and a pot belly
so perfectly round and true it is a thing of beauty
and Chip carves vines and roses, fleurs-de-lis
and hooves of deer for table-legs and turns bright
oak bowls on the lathe, anything really you ask
he will make appear from the grain and he went
to school with me and patiently watches me
struggle with a simple thing and shakes his head.
Says: *Here, try it like this instead*. He is one who
laughs easy, keeps his chisels clean and honed.
How does a man become what he is? Why
is the undertaker an undertaker and the carpet-
layer walking through the world on his knees?
Our mothers, our fathers? A wobble in the stars?
　　　If you are happy in your work,
　　　　　　what is the cause?
Here's another—he too carves like a dream,
mends the broken thing. Almost always quiet,
Wade keeps close to the work at hand and leans
in to see what exactly needs to be done. He is
one to whom I had been cruel once—at least
once, stupid and petty for that is what I am
from time to time. Well, once while living up
in the house by the shop he saw I was working
late in the night and walked through the dark
fields with a plate of venison, carrots and beans
and said *Here, you must be hungry,* and I was.
A broken Windsor chair leaned against the wall.
Steam rose lightly, disappearing as we talked.
The sawdust on my workbench like a tablecloth.

Looking for the Maker's Name

Sometimes on a table like this it is
up underneath. A beautiful thing.
Turn it up over to the left and flip it—
that's good—now set it here straight
down don't pull it along you might
scratch the top. Do you see where
the maker made his name—you can
barely read it—this white chalk across
the pine—can you read that—I can't
either it looks like a J maybe James?
Made just before the Civil War right
around here. It's yellow pine all right.
The grain looks familiar though
probably grew along Piggot's Bottom
where that creek goes catawampus
into the woods probably exactly where
I met my wife—we were standing on
a stump—right beside the road, stars
up in the leaves. Must be the same tree.
Must be. Either that or you are one
gullible fuck. All right then, let's flip
it back on its feet. Easy. Easy! Damn.

At Wartime

Before the signs
  that say God

Loves Dead
  Soldiers and

the loud line
  of motorcycles

revving to end
  the chanting

and before
  the green grass

and the family
  and the bugler

and the body
  underground

and the wound
  there was a man

walking down
  Church Street

with an eyelash
  on his cheek

and no one
  noticed this

detail why
  should we

notice this
  man going

somewhere
  with a lone

eyelash loose
  on his cheek?

Questions I Asked Death, Questions Death Asked Me

Why do you come around here all the time?
  Because the apple trees are bent down low

with fruit and I am hunting like the bee.
  What are you looking for? *A ribbon from*

my mother's hair when she was only three.
  I look in all the robin's nests and I ask

the centipede. What is your real name? *James*
  Edward Smuff the Third, Esquire. Viceroy of

the Cold and the Cobra's Eye, Duke of Blades,
  Bullets and Lord of What Is Broken in the Mind.

Why do you ask? Because my questions are like
  knives and I like waving them in your face.

What are you afraid of exactly? The motionlessness
  of photographs, the quiet of the fair when all

the rides are packed on trucks and pull away
  slowly, the sleeping of the bee and honey

freezing in the hive when winter comes, winter,
  certain snakes, the suffering of those I love.

I could go on. *What are your dreams?* To live
  beyond the days I love and carry you here

on my shoulder. To show you this red ribbon
  I found. To fly. To peacefully grow older.

The Rocking Chair Bookcase

The rocking chair bookcase Chester Cornett built
looks like a throne or the driver's seat of a UFO
that is flown from Kentucky made of black walnut
and hickory cut from the woods and carved to fit—

a rocking chair bookcase—just think of it, all
the books you love rocking with you as you move
a little back and as you move a little frontwards
before the fireplace in the rocking chair bookcase

and no one wants to die and disappear without
a trace and I don't want to live another minute
without a word of praise for the rocking chair
bookcase and the invention of such a thing

Chester Cornett built in 1963 or '62 because
he was a master craftsman and a genius too—
walking in the woods with an ax and an idea
so new it is the meaning of this place where

the invisible leaps out at you and you believe it
and you carve and you carve until you see it and
there it is—the fine-hewn fiddled-with evidence
of grace built by Chester Cornett with the sweat

of his face, this beautiful thing one of the secret
kings of Kentucky made whose lineage may
as well go back to the ones who made fire spin
and the wheel to blaze. O rocking chair bookcase.

Triumph of the Jabberwock
For TWKT

It must be the gimble and the wabe
    and the borogoves out raving.
It must be the nonsense of being
    misbehaving if death is a life.
That must be what it is like.

It must be the silver in the scythe—
    the quick blue winkle in the eye
of the baby born still—stillborn
    beautiful child who will not move
unless we move her body and hold

her body to us. As we do. We move
    as if under water or walking on
the moon so slow it is like a dance.
    Her head lolls back on my hand
and her head lolls back in my hand.

She was born just after she died,
    this reverse life, our life-likeness
who never was long enough to make us
    understand—who we are or why.
Here is the opposite of a lullaby.

When you were invisible I was your
    father and when you are again
unseen I will be again. Nothing
    makes sense. It dips us and leans
as we dance your body here in between.

Phone Call from the Pleistocene

The woman floating downstream on a sycamore tree
    lazy on a hot day escapes her tribe in a cloud
      of mosquitoes and sunshine.

She stinks of prehistory where our ancestors still cut
    their hair with stones and she presses nettles
      to her belly when the baby comes.

Alone by the river miles from the familiar mountains
    and the people she has known she begins our
      beginning as far back as we can trace.

A woman. A river. A breaking. A screaming and then
    a baby in the blood of her lap. Moss makes
      a bed and in the morning we get up.

Time starts its official count and the chromosomes know.
    Look out for the rhinoceros, mother, peeking
      through the ferns. Look out for the lions.

We have a long way to go to get here—a song made
    entirely of prose. A grown man bewildered
      talking with his mother on the phone.

She always says what he needs to be lucky. Of course
    she remembers the panther on the path-way
      and the starfish in the tide pools.

Of course she remembers the bark boat full of strangers
    and the weight of chains. Yes we died, she says,
      but you were never in any danger.

If Faulkner Is Wrong and We Don't Endure or Prevail

Drums for the body desiccated dark down—
way down deep in Mississippi where the silver
wisp of the mustache remains maybe, drums
for the hopeful dreaming and the meaning of
life—what a stupid phrase what a stupid phrase—
drums for the killer and the willing, drums for
the long gone and the still-to-come, drums for
the clothes tattered in the weather—a sweatshirt
maybe that was red and white. Drums for
the body no one has found and drums for
the hair still long along the skull that remains
open from a tire iron or a hammer down,
come-down drums for the shin bone of Beowulf
pocked and slender under the mountain slow
drums for the jaw bone of García Lorca lost
in Spain drums for the box of bones the coroner
sifts through—the cardboard box, the yellowed
broken gnawed-on bones of someone lost
to our humanity come undone or come at last
to its full expression killing the one loved best
or some unlucky one whose death like most
was un-guessed so sudden and so fiercely come,
drums for the dead and gone and all of us
who have come and gone and will continue on.
So the heart drums, the words they come. So
the heart drums, the words they come though
nothing comes—nothing comes—to save you.
Drums for what was beautiful and did no good,
or did just some. Drums for the stupid murderous
ones we always were. Drums for William Faulkner.

2

Pig Fucker's Wife

Is how she signed the beautiful card to Nick
who gave her husband his name long ago
when Josh was a teenager and Pig Fucker

made everyone laugh. And the alternate
names and secret codes of bullshit live on
even though Pig Fucker hasn't worked here

in the shop for years, although we get a card
every year at x-mas from Pig Fucker and Pig
Fucker's wife. And China Boy is as pale and

precious as a china doll and he works now as
a cabinetmaker in Manhattan which sounds
like magic—a cabinetmaker in Manhattan—

and China Boy is a name Chris despises though
it is better than One Eyed Fuck Face and so
China Boy in his turn named someone else

Little Baby Jesus because Little Baby Jesus
was so young and innocent seeming when
he started at the shop and now Baby Jesus

is a librarian somewhere and of course every
cabinet shop in America must have a Malmo,
a Shmendrick, an Opie Dopie and a G. And

an old man named Mr. Martin who lives now
in a Home for years was our upholsterer
hard of hearing who confused the name Kevin

with Cabin and called Kevin Cabin until one day
he could not remember even that though he knew
the name was some kind of homemade thing,

like a lean-to and called him Shack with
a —ck and so we do too today. And many now
are gone like Iron Man, Dude and Drizzle Drip.

Where are you, Drizzle Drip? Your mother can call
you Drew but when you come back to the shop
one day with your beard shaved off and making

lots of money doing something legitimate and show
off your wife and children to us we will greet you
with open arms happy to know you are doing so well.

We are six-tenths of a mile down Allder School
Road over the creek up the washboard road back
in the barn you may remember. Perhaps you have

a name for it—this place that is neither heaven nor hell
where the knuckleheads and hucklebucks remember
you still. This ramshackle shining you once knew well.

Song for the Tribe

When land smashed against land
  and the granite accordion
of the earth's mass moved, it began.

Up went the stones of the mountain.
  Up went the mountain. Up
went the house, up went the city.

And every day since, it is the same.
  Our mothers wake up and up
they rise and out they go laboring

all day until the world is made.
  Our fathers somewhere
sing our secret names, our secret

names, our fathers sing our hidden
  names until the world is made.
Until everyone who is now—is.

Thank you history. Thank you luck—
  thank you all of you who
made us once for we have made

this new one we gaze at all day
  grateful to you—our mothers
and our fathers who somehow

gave him to us though he traveled
  slowly through us rowing slowly
rolling to us in this river in the blood.

The Chisel

For Nick

A walnut handle turned gently
so the butt sets up against
the palm just so and its black
grain is so fine it is like
a sky if the stars are dark
slivers and it is strong, oiled
from use and the steel forged
in Sheffield England early
one morning when the fires
made the iron pour and sway
the way desire shapes us
every day he uses the long
angled silver wedge to say
what needs to be said straight
or rounding to the curving
lay of wood within which
hides the eye of a trout
in the creek-bed watching
as he is found out. A lion's
claw—that sharp and precise.
This tool his grandfather left
with which he's made a life.

Thank-You Wishes for the Wilderness

In a hundred years if all goes well
the house will still stand although
just barely and my three enormous

oak trees will have multiplied and
in a hundred years if all goes well
and wild comes back to the yard

the yard will be what the earth intends—
honeysuckle vines and forest where
the house begins and woods so dense

only rays of light slender as arrows
pierce the canopy and the grandsons
of my rooster fly from branch to branch

hollering in the greeny black leaves of
the evening while my son's grandsons
and their friends run beneath the trees

and no sign of me but them exists and
so thank you wishes for the wilderness—
thank you moon for the silver in the sky,

thank you oaks for the sprawl and climb
you do so well making an architecture
of the air when the first day of autumn

comes and so the first day of autumn
arrives a hundred years before it will
again where the roosters of the future fly

calling to their hens and where my son's
grandsons run through the woods wild
with their homemade knives and their

trouble and their friends and thank you
lord for what never changes but leaves
and falls to rise again for dying never
ends for us. It only slowly rearranges us.

Death of a Unicorn

No one believes in unicorns but there it was—
    dead on the road with seven buzzards
landing hard beside the bloat and frenzy
    of the little white beetles in the body
and the black hooves and eyes wide open

and the buck must have lost its other horn
    long ago so only one straight prong grew
and all four legs were broken too, its head
    thrown back by the force of the truck that
smashed through the apparition last night

and the girl in the garden of Eden feels a chill
    suddenly as the sun goes down the first time.
And the girl in the house beside the road who
    saw the deer for days grazing in the field
sleeps unknowing still. And the girl in the truck

who died last night flies south in the same
    path she took from the windshield and is
now gliding over the suburbs of Memphis
    four hundred miles away, the rising sun
drying her tears and the girl in the wagon

with her hair cut off stares at the guillotine
    and the girl stunned between the second boy
and the third and the girl whose father lifts
    the body of the deer with a backhoe all
grow souls like muscles—alive—alive-oh.

The Cabinetmaker's Window

Honing his chisel in the figure-eight.
Doing an actual jitterbug with
Mr. Martin on the oak floor upstairs
because we wanted to see what
exactly it looked like. Drinking

a little dandelion wine just because
we made it ourselves everybody
on their knees one spring day picking
the golden flower from the fields.
Honing his chisel in the figure-eight.

Planing walnut so the purple shows.
Carving pins for the tenons and then
banging them home when the table is
done—just so an eighth pokes out.
Cutting his hand suddenly on the saw

bleeding in the room where the smell
of blood grows faint as the day goes on.
Measuring by eye, measuring by tape.
Taking a minute to look out the window.
Honing his chisel in the figure-eight.

Like OMG, I Can Die Now ♥ Pammy

(Like Oh-My-Shiz) Dear God.
Two words: Backstreet Boys.
            —pammysixteen.blogspot.com

If you don't mind dying suddenly
painlessly instantly then your happiness
now must be enormous as the sun,
your joy as round as the Roman Coliseum
every day like the fantastical gift
breath is giving and never taking away.

If you don't mind disappearing now
from the planet, from the fine rub
of the inside of your clothes, from the kiss
of your beloved and the dream turning
in your head turning to bliss then
you are happier now than you ever were.

You are so content you are like a butternut
squash in the fat shade of your leaves.
You are the goat untethered wandering
the rocky side of the mountain yelling
short loud announcements to the pines
and the wolves and your happiness

defies the sharp teeth of the mountain
defies the scythe of the moon and the dark
dropping down of the robes of the night
and you are so ready now, so happy
words are starting to fail and you let them.
    You let the world at last go silent.

Ars Aureus

First was the golden horse shit,
    those clumps of grassy dough
I picked up with a shovel
    in my neighbor's meadow.

One dollar an hour at least
    and it took me a few hours
a day to pick up after the mares
    and stallions who'd watch me

as I wheeled the barrow
    here and there and shoveled in
the tufty dirty loaves of seeds
    and oats and one afternoon

kneeling in the pasture with
    all of the horses watching
and whisking their long tails
    in the summer heat I took

a golden seed out of the earth
    of the horse and rubbed it
clean and said the blessing of
    thanks I learned from my family

for the unbroken unity of all
    things and it was sweet,
surprisingly sweet, as it is
    today, reading and writing
poetry doing the work I love.

Lines for the Atrium of a High School

The boy in the hallway knows the wonder of imagination.
　　How it turns the trees to young women at night where
he can walk among them and feel their leaves graze his face

as he walks beneath. He is perhaps sixteen when he sees it:
　　light pooling in the little bowl of the collarbone of a girl
walking through the hallway of the school. Brass trophies

shine in the morning light that pours from the garden of
　　pine trees and irises outside the tall windows. And here
she comes—a girl maybe fifteen with light across her neck

and two friends on either side all laughing at something as
　　the crowds of teenagers pass each other giddy in their
despairs before the day begins. The image of light filling

the scooped-out place of the girl's collarbone is just that.
　　An image, a detail. He moves along and the days course
onward like some ordinary river, like a sentence, the one

he is writing today with nothing before him but the changing
　　light of noon. Such light has a thousand ways of being
discovered, of being described. Some of them might endure

the night. For the boy one illuminates still. It illuminates
　　and illuminates. So what if two people marry and live
a long life together? So what such light illuminates still?

After Ammianus of the 2nd Century A.D.

Dawn after dawn slips past us unremarked.
Sky with an eagle in the white cloud.
Sky with a jet. Sky so low and white
with fog to move at all is to loom

like a cyclops and lump through the yard.
Dawn after dawn a darker blue gives way
to the lighter shades until it bleaches
into noon and the saws of the shop all stop.

The quiet of noon is about a second long,
something between Holy and Fuck, or,
the distance between the turning of a key
and the roar and purr of a diesel truck.

One afternoon a thousand green caterpillars
of the Luna Moth came to eat the broad
leaves of the catalpa and you could hear
their jaws working still when the moon rose.

We did remark that. Evening after evening
comes on and the light of the day falls back
to blue and that blue grows deep and wide.
At three in the morning the table-saw blade

finally cools and the quiet gets used to itself.
Mice run across the hammers and a black
snake follows the slowest one home—her
long body winding silently over the claws.

Song for the Carry-On

In the minute and a half it takes
    for a plane to fall from the sky
there is time to pray for all of us
    living now who will in this way
die the excruciating slow fall of

strangers cloud-high and plunging
    down together and there is time
while the lights flicker and the fire
    grows and the human noise stuns
everyone and all certainty disappears

except for the impending one now
    rising up like cornfields or cities
to snatch us back—there is still
    a moment or two in the chaos of
gravity to say something—it's OK—

It's OK.
    Once as a boy my father helped
a sheep give birth and the thing was
    stuck and so he put his hand inside
the body and pulled out a thick bouquet

of flowers—tulips, roses and a spray
    of Queen Anne's lace. He was a boy.
He told me this when I was grown,
    old enough to know better. It's ok.
Breath carries us and we fall away.

Driving Around

For two years he lasted picking up the bodies
of deer blasted into pieces on the roadside
raccoons, possums, cats, an occasional
vulture or goose, birds more fleet having air
to rise into. Mostly it was earthbound ones
filled with worms, bug-eyed, the carcass moving
with the force of what is hungry inside never
minding him too much hoisting everything up
into the bed of the truck. He lasted two years.
A white dog unharmed it seemed sleeping still
by the roadside undid him. Lifting its body
lolling and still warm he placed it on the seat
beside him as he drove home trailing the stink
of his work through town and buried the animal
in his front yard, three quartz stones as big as
skulls to mark the place. Look, we just passed it.
Let me back up. No I didn't say *dog*. It was a boy.
Neighbors saw him bury him in the plain of day.
Neighbors saw the cops and what they say is
he killed the boy and buried him and came
loose with a hatchet at the law. I don't know.
You could hear the blam-blam-blam a mile away.
My brother loved his wife and his boy, both.
There are many things that are never ok. Most.
Don't ever tell me anything is ok. Don't ever
tell me nothing. You can get out here and walk.

3

The Little Girl from Outer Space

To Lady Wonton Bianca—a racehorse
who never won a thing—was born
a half-lame quarter horse with a horn.

Nothing special. Nothing special but
a half-lame quarter horse with a horn
we love to feed apples to and call Silver

Queen and Your Majesty because she
is fine to look at and limps like magic
that is worn down a little and broken

which is what we are I guess and that
is enough. That is enough to live by
a while which is how it came to pass

that my friend walked through the dusty
sunlight of 3 p.m. in the cabinet shop
today with liquor on his breath

and sawdust flecked in his beard
and half of a finger chopped off from
long ago and wired with a native joy

that gallops inside him he grabbed
two pieces of carved maple meant for
a chair and stood between them as if

they were two golden scepters and said
in a high falsetto the dogs could hear
I am just a little girl from outer space!

and danced a little shuffle standing
in place for the meaning of life must
be spoken sometimes with a perfect

straightness of the face. It is nothing.
It is nothing. It will always be nothing.
Dumb-luck whiskey wonder and grace.

On the Back of an Envelope

The secret he wrote was
I will never die.

Around him the springtime
burst into green

laughter and blossoms
faded and fell to the ground.

It had nothing to do with him.
In the valley of the shadow

of death one fears
all manner of things all the time:

the man with a knife,
the haunted word,

armies moving in the dead
of night. The secret

of life, whatever that is,
carries him onward

plunging through the redbud trees
like a god—toward his death.

The Denunciation of Ricky Skaggs
from On High

No more light strumming of your mandolin
and the whispered tone and the sap-
happy featherweight songs in my honor.

Ricky, no more treacly bullshit. I actually
rose up from the dead. Do you understand
what that means exactly? A god. A mother-

trucking god is who you are singing to. Did
Zeus get tickled with a zither and prance
on his tippy-toes like a poodle someone

shaved? No. Did my Father get weepy little
valentines and thank-you notes for nothing
but pain and suffering for a thousand years?

He got hollering and screams and fists raised
at the sky. He got rockabilly eventually and
heavy metal and thrash. Listen to Bill Monroe.

He won't just kiss my ass. Ricky you have
suffered in your life enough to know better
than to sing that stuff. It pains me to hear it.

Stick to what hurts most and mean it. Cut open
something valuable and bleed it. Hang it
upside down in your yard and let it drain

into the grass. My god Ricky I might have to
come down there and show you what I mean.
Don't make me. I have eyes like laser beams

and a voice like Ralph Stanley but deeper
down darker. No more sweetness Ricky.
You are not a bee. There is a broken-down

burning house inside the soul and someone
in the window waves. It is me. Dammit
Ricky, do something. Sing something true

the way you used to. Heaven is not a given.
Make a ladder of what actually happens
to matter to you—blood, strings and the ear.

Days We Can't Play Black Sabbath

When the power goes he rolls the Victrola
to the center of the floor and it squats
there like a primitive robot ready to go.
Rain pours or flies sideways at the barn
where we work and lightning cracks
blue W's above us but we don't mind.

Work by the windows. Carve in the light
the rain can't stop. Sweat a little more.
Instead of the radio and the wilderness
of voices we are most of the time—now
it is the murmur of work and Todd
changing records on his own Victrola.

He loves it you know. Rebuilt it, saved it
from ruin for a while and made it shine.
The big shellac '78s are heavy and round.
He plays the crank and lets it fly all day
if the wires are down. Louis Armstrong
blows the thunder around and you can

hear the gold in the horn. Dance a little
if you like or sing along. Make fun of it
or scream for someone please to turn it
down—whatever—you can't ignore it.
Out there in the skinny meadow the mule
can hear it when we open the doors. This
calling so loud it's brother to the storm.

Ode with a Dolphin at the End

Mostly thanking winter is pleasure for the spring.
Mostly thanking cold is knowing the heat
in things—how it kindles and carries on.

Mostly thanking death is mercy for our pain.
The homicidal maniac who sleeps inside
our blood eventually gets up and wakes

his brothers and his sisters and so the body
becomes a city of murder and cruelty
without end until the End. Archways of

the body where they pass in the darkness
toward the square—knives glinting, eyes
shot through with ice green as pines. Oh

terrible city in which we crumble. Mostly
being humble was knowledge of our limits.
Mostly I'm afraid the winter comes to stay.

Thank you snow for melting and earth
for turning closer to the sun. Thank you
mind of mine for abstraction, for the story

the springtime tells every year telling me
death is something passing we survive.
Thanking death for anything mostly is a lie.

Thank you death for deceit and the holiness
of words and the animal leaping in the sky
now returning to the water and leaping
    up again now moving toward the water.

On the Birth of a Friend's Child

Among the noises of the slaughterhouse
    everyone is blinking—
a calf leaping in the trough.

Under the Collard Greens and the Poppies

White Kitty, Gray Kitty, Singie and Lee,
   Roughass, Christos, Caledonia and Getz,
Heather and Puffy, Bullet and Bunky

   Liza and Carrie, Cutie and Myette.
Of approximately thirty shop cats
   over the years only four are left.

Scooter is alive but Dickie is dead.
   And Carrie lives but a tumor points
out of her head and she walks like

   a coon and shambles toward death.
Same for Arnie and Beth the foxes
   got and Li'l Bastard too we guess

who must have been tough to chew
   and Altie was hit by a car which is
the most common of all ways to die,

   his fat plush body still warm when
we found him and Alotta Sweetness,
   Alotta Sweetness so suddenly so

mysterious last year just fell over
   and today the fat three-legged one
we called Precious Darling—and called

   Peachy too because Precious Darling
was so embarrassing to say—has died of
   old age who had only three legs to leap

and grip the earth and catch mice with
    and did—roaming under the barn during
thunder storms arriving later in the arms

    of Hot Toddy who loved her and loves
all of the shop cats and feeds them special
    crunchies from a jar and speaks to them

with tenderness every day until they die
    and buries them in the garden under
the collard greens and the poppies

    and the honeydew melons white
as moons so every night in the dark of
    death the garden's darling tigers bloom.

To a Cloud over Troy

Unvoiced and overlooked
   by Virgil and Homer
who scoured the ruins
   of the city for significance
and glory—this cloud

scarcely more than words
   of white floats in the air
over Troy trailing a little
   downward falling like smoke
from a chimney in the sky

equally invisible—the fire
   not of gods nor of men,
it flickers above them
   high above the lineage
of the gods and above

our ideas of the eternal,
   unvoiced and overlooked
which is its nature
   and from which we take
our portion returning to it

at last—this pleasure
   that is not pleasure
but its absence—being
   forgotten eventually for
even the ghost grows old

and dissolves in the air
   and the dinosaur lies down
lost in the mud and blinks—
   her body a stillness now.
Beauty without significance.

Dreaming Made the Hula Hoop

From the language of the first tribe
dhreugh—meaning to deceive—became
dream and the blessed wheel of nights

turning to days now turning to night
rolls onward still and it is difficult
to believe but every one of the billions

of us breathing and walking
on the planet turning beneath us
are cousins enough we can see

ourselves in one another's faces
and one of us long ago cut a switch
of maple and made a circle lashed

at the ends with grass and invented
the hula hoop and grooved anciently
in her furs and everyone I'm sure

wanted one and later the wheel
followed and dreaming made
the hula hoop and dreaming gave

shape to everything that moved
like the planets in their faraway
roundabout Copernican grooves

and the honeybee's erratic dance
map of moves that tells where
the flowers are and dreaming

made the heavens shine so dying
was the dream and dying was
the lie and dying died at least

for a while in the holy books
and in the mind and though
we are dying all the time, dying

all the time, even though we are
dying all the time someone
moves her hips in a roundabout

defiant line somewhere we least
expect—a graveyard in Kentucky,
or the nursing home's dark hall.

Whose granddaughter is this? Who
moves in every cell of the body
that eventually gradually falls?

You Should, Said Socrates, Sing a Charm over Him
Everyday Until You Have Charmed Away His Fears
—Plato, *Phaedo*

The skeleton of a cobra, the tooth of St. Paul,
the bright blue tunic of Sappho and the mirror
in the hall of a house in Pompeii. The dark red

clay of a bowl here holds two pomegranates
and a pear. The wonders of the world include
these and Kathleen my children and the oak trees

that lean over the house and the reader unseen
and the writer unseen and this scrap of words
sung in between. What will be done with all

the life we will leave? What is it we become?
The skeleton of a cobra, a mastodon's tongue,
the archway of a cathedral, a song sung

only once and the crack of the rung when
someone enters paradise. The dark red clay
of this bowl my friend made rests on the table

and it rests on the table all day never moving
though I won't take my eyes away. I won't
move an inch. Let everything stay this way

a little longer and we'll make it through.
Every day I get up and say it over and over,
    this charm for what rises in me like a cobra.

Music for the Word *Perhaps*

The star in the furnace
   and the myrrh in the mind
go softly through the lazy, lord,
   go softly through the mind.

In Delaware the elephants
   kneel down for you to ride.
With a sash and a ruby go
   gently through the mind.

Go rollercoaster-slow lord
   and swing out like a tassel.
Five long white cranes
   float over the castle

of my body as your hand
   comes down from the sky.
Go softly through the lazy,
   softly through the mind.

What is love but a Tuesday
   setting fire to the flood? Go
softly through the flames, lord,
   moving through the blood.

The Hillbilly Break-Dance and the Talking Crow

So the school bus skids around the mountain and kills
my friend's dog almost instantly and Lester in the back seat
sticks his face out the window to say "Don't eat that dog,
he's dead meat" and laughs and that was long ago and Lester

lives in the mountain ghetto where the rich have not yet
ruined the land with their paper mansions and he is hillbilly
wild as a teenager and learns to break-dance and locks
and pops and turns and rocks like a robot on summer nights

drunk under the Christmas lights of his back porch where
we watch as Lester works through his routine and once
he moon-walked right off the edge and dropped down
hard into the honeysuckle and the blue rocks of the place

and sprung back to his feet and said "I'm all right god dammit"
and shinnied back up to move some more and so it is not
hard to believe Lester banged out of his house last week
bored on a Sunday afternoon in August and wandered in

the woods of the mountain as if through some cathedral
so dark with leaves and fiddlehead ferns that light only
reaches the ground through a thousand little tunnels and
suddenly at his feet hop-hop-hopping along comes a crow

who says *all right then, all right, how are you?* and Lester
stops. *All right then, how are you?* says the crow again and
cocks its head and looks up with its beady eye at Lester
who looks away. Trucks rumble down the mountain hard

in the distance and an airplane starts to make a sharp curve
a mile above but they don't know anymore about the world
for a minute, Lester and the crow talking a while, he says just
shooting the breeze. He says that crow knew the names of his

father and his grandfather and "all kinds of personal shit"
and it said *Lester, look at you. You've grown middle-aged
and fat but I like you anyways* and flew back into the trees
just to let him think about it. And six other people have

talked to this crow and now it is legend and that is why
I am sitting in the Mount Hebron cemetery with a picnic
lunch and waiting while the story does its thing I guess
flying from tree to tree chasing owls maybe looking

for something shiny which is why I have lined up ten
dimes and a safety pin on the stone wall. To attract some
magic, to call down the blessing of an impossible thing.
All right then. It is getting darker. Let the new life begin.

4

Whiskey for Sorrow and a Song of Disgrace

He is buried standing so you can see his face

jut from the ground in the rock of the place.

This farm must have once been his, perhaps

it still is. Wind moves the hay like waves

around him and sometimes we eat lunch

up there sprawled around him. He looks

like a dead king in his green glass case.

The knots of his ears like relics of a saint.

When we are gone all of this will change.

It has already. Houses rise from bulldozer

blades until all the land is laid to waste.

There should be a reckoning for the ruin,

a sword of fire, a plague. All we have is

whiskey for sorrow and a song of disgrace.

There should be a temple here and pine

boughs for the bones of the genius of place.

The Laborer

First it whirs
   like magic so
he can't believe
   a chunk of oak
once quiet sky-
   high lost in
the woods is
   now this hurry
that spins blurry
   before him
at the lathe,
   this rattling-
faster-than-
   breathing- or-
thinking-lathe
   that is always
quick as dream
   this technology,
quiet as a horse-
   fly sighing, spins
while someone
   with a chisel
powering into it
   leans and little
light sparks of
   oak arc in the air
or else he only
   just touches
the thing like flying
   touches the wing
and a bowl comes
   into view or
rounds and coves
   of a chandelier

or spokes to
    a Windsor chair,
some loveliness
    you have to dream
before it's there
    like coolness of
the night air
    above the trees
or the name of
    your bride, so
he works at
    the lathe
and the lathe
    works on him
in the careful way
    labor clarifies.
It is the why.
    It is the growl
and purl of making,
    almost though
never breaking,
    the burl and limb,
work's master hymn
    that shapes him.

What Sings in the Garden Shines in the Sun

The paint-can robot somebody built I don't know
how or why but it came with the house and it rules
the world of the garden and the pleasant half-acre

behind the house standing shining among the green
beans and tomatoes and the corn standing shining
in the summer heat reflecting light like a bonfire, or

in the falling rain drumming to make a heartbeat
for all of the town to hear, standing in the snow
and fog—its dark eyes punched through by an awl

perhaps forty years ago and the jagged mouth
cut with a hacksaw or tin-snips for the maw
within which a wren has found her way to nest

for generations now her family filling the bucket
head with yellow straw, twigs and long strands of
horsehair and the silver of someone gone and so

she flies in and out of the mouth today like a small
speech the robot makes and I think of the loneliness
of the soul inside the body and how it must be

in there—pushing the sticks around, watching out
for crows, hunting the ladybug and the night-crawler
flying around alone while the paint-can robot sings

in the garden saying only what the wren says with
her wings: I'm going, I'm home, I'm going, I'm home.
All day long—the paint-can robot scarecrow's song.

The Way the Days Pass One after Another

Is the way water falls in a glassy sheet over rocks
    when the river is low and stepping down through
the valley and the way the word *divine* is written
    slowly in a man's notebook where the ink shines
a moment and the way ten thousand feathers

of a wild turkey go together over the river moving
    south and the static on the radio and all the elements
of a sadness you cannot escape when you think
    of death and the abstract new ache of middle age
and you might hope the fragments of a long sentence

add up to something you can say out loud and be
    calmed and soothed by knowing the list and timbre
of words matter in the small room of your making
    where the moon shines a moment and a true rhyme
clicks like a heavy door and some redneck drunk on

gasoline hollers your name as he drives by and soon
    the people you know will no longer be and so I return
to this subject sad so constantly that I drink whiskey
    and listen to the mountain get in the way of the AM
station in Front Royal whose white noise is fine tonight

like the river's quiet passage from one place to another
    that is always going-on and always going-on must
be so ancient a feeling it is the thing divine the word
    was caused to be—and it rises in the air and moves
across the land devouring devouring and devouring.

Thank You Lord for the Dark Ablaze—

For the deer gut busted open splayed
on the gravel margin of the highway
to remind me and to horrify which are
the same when death comes to say
anything for dying is a song the body
is learning so thank you lord for this
enduring whir of days we ride the way
a chisel carves down deep as it glides
for being is a lathe and we are the turning
curving shape of what I come to praise
so thank you Lord for the edge of light
when the day is honed and all is bright
behind the eyes just before waking for
dream is a fire we are the lake of—
dream is the spire we are the church
of—and the days turn so fast meaning
rattles hard and nearly breaks off—so
thank you lord for what arrives today
crashing down without a warning like
a pick-up truck on the deer this morning
or the morning light lashing me while
the sun flickers churning through the trees
like a wheel splashing rays on the redbud
dappling this holy thing I stand beneath
and I stand beneath and that is all, for
green is the mind of the spring returning
and dying a song the body is learning
which I will not sing or step to although
every day—oh—that is exactly what I do.

How the Things We Work On, Work On Us

A blue horse from a carousel in Atlantic City stood looking shocked on the barn floor for days, the wind moving through its poplar mane. A thousand rickety Windsor chairs, tables and dressers and secret boxes of mahogany, rosewood and pearl. We've worked on half of the objects ever made in the world is how it feels though it must be more. Walnut four-paneled eight-foot doors, a mirror Jefferson gazed back at, bookcases that twirl, wardrobes and canes. Ten thousand times a thousand things made badly or with genius have passed through this place, each one its own special challenge, its own set of troubles. Everything busted by hard use. Farm tables grooved by the butcher's knife, tables marred with bloodstains, scorch marks, or water. Sewing machines from Singer, Victrolas and violas busted open and bared, all of it smashed and ruined and fallen out of use by neglect and disrepair and the shit of creatures that lurk wherever Grandmother's father's things are stored. Two carved lions on a Morris chair roar. Roll-top desks fall apart on the floor. The pretty olive-wood head of an eighteenth-century girl stares out the window, her slender nose broken. Here is a commode from Florence, a cedar trunk from Rome, the strange furnishings of a home. When you walk in the front door of our shop, stairs jump up and if you happen to look in the air as you climb you will see an enormous oak eagle with a broken claw hovering above you. It has been there for years. And the chair Frederick Douglass sat in while working at his desk was here all summer. We did very little with it, repaired a caster, waxed it. Walking by, I liked to caress the canvas where his back would rest, where his scarred back would lean lightly and rest. He knew how things persist. I'm learning. The ordinary is always a sacred object.

On the Rebel Flag over
My Neighbor's House

Yes indeed fly it proudly.
There is no reason
to take it down—your flag
of defeat, blood and treason.
I drag it here along the ground.

To the Cabinetmakers

In my dream of the shop the ceilings are low
and the barn leans into the western wind

like a ship through the Straits of Magellan
and the straight line where the grass meets

the hay is as clear as a latitudinal line
although the hay now is high as waves

an ocean makes after a storm and whales
surface and dive back down and I see

the dream in the morning and I see it
all day at the shop planing maple for a bed

or clamping oak veneer to a tabletop and
I can feel waves rock the barn and the slip-

slop passage of blood in my body for
the shop is a ship and we go out to sea

every morning sharpening our knives,
loading rum by rolling barrels up a long

pine plank into the belly of the boat
we love to sail through Virginia up

over the mountains into West Virginia
and out westward over the hills of waves

and the stars at night grow deep as lanterns
and someone sleeps in the crow's nest

to see what he can see, someone always
sleeps on the roof of the sea dreaming

his way through another day that is
ordinary and otherworldly, always in

the valley of a wave going up and over.
No wonder a cabinetmaker might

cut his finger off or lurch into the walls.
No wonder we come here every day.

Song for Sunday Morning

The dolphin in the woods
  leaps from tree to tree
and is only wind is only
  the yellow of poplar leaves

and the blue of September
  where the little windows are.
Everyday our fathers live
  they breathe the air that was

something else in another time.
  If the atom is to be believed
we all shift and change.
  What was the river becomes

the cloud. What we wanted
  to say we never could.
It was obvious. It was hidden
  like the dolphin in the woods.

Poem Ending with a Line from Auden

(May 1, 2012)

From what I can gather tonight
  paging through the onion-skin
paper of my dictionary there are
  three meanings for the tribal
Indo-European root of the word
  magic (which is *magh*) and they

are: one, to be able; two, to fight;
  and three, a young person, and if
you put all three together you see
  the painted face of a boy holding
the serene expression of one about
  to slaughter something or to take

the sharpened end of a spear through
  his neck and the birch leaves
fluttering behind him won't help
  and the clouds moving slowly over
won't help and the stones piled
  up at his feet won't help unless

someone says the marshaling noise
  of luck and sings the protecting
songs that make the granite chunk
  fit the warrior's hand just so
to fly to the mark and make clouds
  move from the sun just enough

to blind and bewilder the enemy
  across the field also blessed by
songs of their own sung a little
  differently as the leaves
of the trees flutter and stones fly
  and the young men, able, run by.

From what I can gather tonight
    magic may be nothing but prayer
and poetry a working knowledge
    of lies. As Auden said once
in 1939 and then took it back—
    we must love one another or die.

The Taste of It

The taste of it like lake water in paradise
her nipple swirling like a chocolate
in the mouth, the bump of it like blood
coursing in the body, what you guess

when thrust meets thrust in the darkness.
What tastes plain somehow like the air
when you gasp, the reaching back to days
on days that blur with plenitude so that

the details and the sorrow and the nail
you stepped on disappear and it is only
blue sky and the stars you can taste—
knowing what you've always wanted

has come and sizzles on the tongue.
This thing that is so difficult to name—
this sting of flame that never hurt me.
The taste of water when you are thirsty.

In the Parking Lot of the Barbershop

I come from a long line of jackass halfwits
stumbling toward America forever
     until one fell into the broad cleavage
of the customs officer's bride
     on Ellis Island in the summertime.

It was the Atomic Age until we spoke
in anything but a broken way—
     our hands waving at the world.
I come from a long line of angry
     chimney sweeps and drunken barbers.

Men with tongues as smooth as mirrors
and women wild as hope
     as one thing slowly led to another:
our traditional cursings of god
     leading to a begging for mercy.

I come from a long line of the dead
now collected in one place—the hold
     of a ship lost at sea in a storm
that makes me dizzy. My skull
     aches and I know they are in there.

If someone punched me in the nose
they would fall out of their chairs.
     I come from a long line of dabblers,
cobblers and hunchbacks,
     delusional mooks and fools.

I come from the swirling lights of
the barbershop wanting to cry
     right there in the parking lot.

Big open-faced crying in the parking lot.
  Oh children, look at us—

No matter what our hair sticks up
and there was never any reason
  for love. You can wonder
why you were born and who
  you are and I'll tell you this—

you come from the parking lot and
the factory and days so hot the air
  shimmers and nights as cool
as the cottonmouth of a snake.
  We came from nothing one day:

A fish, a protozoan, a lightning strike
suddenly in the dead calm of a lake.
  The jagged line of brightness
time is—started everything to move
  toward the drawing of a breath.

And the drawing of your mother
someone did years ago, and which
  we see everyday in the hall,
still shines. We come from sleep
  every morning and see it is true.

We carved toothpicks from pine
trees for the captains of industry.
  We killed thousands. We died.
We mumblers and mouth-breathers,
  humdingers and breeders.
            We'll be fine.

ACKNOWLEDGMENTS

Grateful acknowledgment is made to the editors of the following journals, where the works listed first appeared: *ABZ Press*: "After Ammianus of the 2nd Century A.D.," "Ars Aureus," "Song for Sunday Morning" (as "Diving through the Forest"), "Thank You Lord for the Dark Ablaze—," "To a Cloud over Troy," and "Whiskey for Sorrow and a Song of Disgrace"; *Cortland Review*: "In the Parking Lot of the Barbershop" and "Under the Collard Greens and the Poppies"; *Hopkins Review*: "The Hillbilly Break-Dance and the Talking Crow," "The Rocking Chair Bookcase," and "Triumph of the Jabberwock"; *Iron Horse*: "The Chisel" and "The Laborer"; *Oxford American*: "The Denunciation of Ricky Skaggs from On High"; *Poetry International*: "Song for the Carry-On"; *Shenandoah:* "The West Virginia Copper-Wing"; *32 Poems*: "Pig Fucker's Wife," "Questions I Asked Death, Questions Death Asked Me," and "The Taste of It"; *Writer's Chronicle*: "If Faulkner Is Wrong and We Don't Endure or Prevail."

"Triumph of the Jabberwock" and "Song for the Carry-On" were published in a letter-press edition chapbook by Q Avenue Press in 2013.

"You Should, Said Socrates, Sing a Charm over Him Every Day Until You Have Charmed Away His Fears" was commissioned by Michael Keller's Abaculi Project.

❧

"Phone Call from the Pleistocene" is for my mother.
"Lines for the Atrium of a High School" is for Kathleen.
"The Laborer" is in memory of Jack Lancto.
"What Sings in the Garden Shines in the Sun" is for Ross Gay.
"Song for Sunday Morning" is for my father and grandfather.
"In the Parking Lot of the Barbershop" is for Terrance Hayes.

❧

The first line of "After Ammianus of the 2nd Century A.D." is taken from Sherod Santos's *Greek Lyric Poetry*.

Great thanks to my family for their support and to the poets Leslie Shiel, Ross Gay, Susan Varnot, Paul Gibbons, and Dave Smith for their careful reading and encouragement. As ever, thanks to Nick Greer and his Antiques Conservation Shop.

CPSIA information can be obtained
at www.ICGtesting.com
Printed in the USA
LVHW100121150223
739488LV00004B/773

9 780807 154496